ELECTRIC SNAKES

BOOKS BY ADRIAN C. LOUIS

POETRY
The Indian Cheap Wine Séance (1974)
Muted War Drums (Chapbook, 1977)
Sweets for the Dancing Bears (Chapbook, 1979)
Fire Water World (1989, 2013)
Among the Dog Eaters (1992, 2013)
Days of Obsidian, Days of Grace (1994)
Blood Thirsty Savages (1994)
Vortex of Indian Fevers (1995)
Ceremonies of the Damned (1997)
Skull Dance (Chapbook, 1998)
Ancient Acid Flashes Back (2000)
Bone & Juice (2001)
Evil Corn (2004)
Deer Dreams (Chapbook, 2006)
Logorrhea (2006)
Archeology (Chapbook, 2011)
Savage Sunsets (2012)
Random Exorcisms (2016)
Electric Snakes (2018)

FICTION
Skins (1995, 2002)
Wild Indians & Other Creatures (1996)

EDITOR
Shedding Skins: Four Sioux Poets (2008)

ELECTRIC SNAKES

Poems

Adrian C. Louis

The Backwaters Press

The Backwaters Press
1124 Pacific Street, #8392
Omaha, NE, 68108
(402) 451-4052

The Backwaters Press

Published 2018 by The Backwaters Press

Louis, Adrian C.
        Electric Snakes / Adrian C. Louis.
        ISBN-10: 1-935218-91-3
        ISBN-13: 978-1-935218-91-3 (pb)
        Library of Congress Control Number: 2017939985

Typesetting by Steve Foley
The text of this book is set in Adobe Garamond Pro.

First Edition

Printed in the United States of America

For Colleen

Now, nearly all those I loved and did not understand when I was young are dead, but I still reach out to them.

—Norman Maclean

The world of men is dreaming.
It has gone mad in its sleep,
and a snake is strangling it,
but it can't wake up.

—D.H. Lawrence

ACKNOWLEDGMENTS

Several poems in this collection were published previously, some in earlier versions, in *New Letters, Copper Nickel, South Dakota Review, Main Street Rag, Petrichor, San Pedro River Review, I-70 Review, Plume, Bat City Review, Pouch, Indian Country Today, Chiron Review, Red Ink, Turtle Island Quarterly, Fried Chicken & Coffee, Ask Yourself, Superstition Review, Tammy, Dead Inside: Zombie Poems, The Meadow, Lana Turner, Talking River Review, North American Review, Mojave River Review, Natural Bridge, Raleigh Review,* and *What Saves Us: Poems of Empathy & Outrage in the Age of Trump.* Thanks bigly to all the extremely discerning editors of these publications.

Sincere appreciation to Michael Catherwood and Greg Kosmicki and their crew at The Backwaters Press in Omaha. Thanks also to Trevino Brings Plenty and Sky Hopinka for the noble savagery of their artful assistance. *Pesa u.*

CONTENTS

ELECTRIC SNAKES

When I Was a Zombie

A dusty snow in Santa Fe.
In a cracked adobe bungalow
on a nameless backstreet
a pot of beans was boiling.
"Not for me," I said & ate her
wet brain until arid jellyfish
flew from my eyes. When I
heard her baby cry, I put
on my jacket & booked.
This was during my
no-good years & years
before I would admit
I had once
been that baby.

How a Poem Is Born

The phone rings. I never answer without
first checking the caller ID. The caller ID
flashes my name & number—hey WTF?
How the holy hell's such a thing possible?
Curiosity almost trumps fear, but in the
end I do not answer. No message is left.
My stomach is still fluttering. What if
I answered & I was on the other end?
What could I say? "Dick with me &
I will definitely double-dick you."
Of course we'd have to sit & wait
for the magic blue pills to paint red
the sky above the dueling ground.

Pussy Karma

It was a large house, white paint peeling, perched
upon beams stouter than any made these days.
One day two scraggly cats appeared, drank from
the gift of a saucer of canned milk & vanished.
Then some months later six plump & fluffy
kittens crawled from beneath the ancient house.
Six became sixty & sixty became six hundred
but at least they did not shit in the house.
They found their way back underneath
the house & shit to their hearts' content.
A mountain grew under the house, taller
& taller until its anchoring spikes snapped
& the house broke free from its mooring &
still it rose, a white house in white clouds,
perched precariously on a mountain of shit.

Applause

Thanks to advanced age,
I am now a card-carrying
member of the American
Federation of Asshats.
So, this fine winter morn,
I shambled on down to
Wally World & bought
a "clap on, clap off" lamp.
Tonight, in my lonely bed,
I applauded the chilled
darkness & it vanished.
I was bathed in the birth
of pallid, yellow light.
Bored with muttering
to my ancient shadow
on the wall, I applauded
lightly & I vanished into
cold, dark night to dance
with the dear demons
of those I so loved.

The Multiverse

I see a snowy world beyond
my Kmart Venetian blinds.
The guy I hire to snow-blow
my sidewalk has fallen twice.
After the second fall, he digs
inside his parka & retrieves
a shiny pint of Jack Daniel's.
I once had his altered gravity.
But do the snowflakes come
by gravity or by a furious
desire to kiss the cold earth?
Godless scientists now go
door to door proclaiming
that we live in a Multiverse.
I think that means beyond
our universe lies another &
beyond that one another & so
on until the cows come home.
A gazillion worlds, multiversal
dudes *ad infinitum,* shit-faced
& stumbling, cursing softly
their snow-blowing lives.

Otter Girl

My dopey dick droops
even further when I note
your hands on your hips
& those hips shaking dozens
of metal cones into tiny clattering
prayers for those in need of healing.
Your jingle side-step is holy, but holy
damn. Beneath the shimmering green
of the dress, your brown, rippling otter
flesh is muscled & pouring sweat & darling
for a few feeble moments I am healed &
visibly younger & not some gray haze
sleepwalking upon this dying earth.

What the Older Boys Told Me

Ah, but I was so much older then.
I'm younger than that now.
　　—Bob Dylan

They told me if I soaked my agates in milk
overnight, the half moons would vanish.
Though they phrased it more crudely,
they said if I were the first to open a peach
& drink the sweet juices, the pink ghost
of that peach would hover eternally
in the small sky between my shoulders.

At Jimmy John's

I have driven through
Jimmy John's every day
for the past eight days,
always the same time,
always the same order.
Three oatmeal cookies,
a small Fanta Orange
& some extra napkins.
I am sick of the cookies,
but the beautiful Chicana
at the register now calls
me "Señor Cookie Man."
Such a pretty girl with such
splendiferous back acreage.
Today when I got my change I
said, "Thanks, for everything."
She smiled widely. I melted.
For an oddly eternal moment,
I was a quivering boy in
an old man's body.

Easter Egg

Today I boiled an egg
& hid it in my yard
so that tomorrow I
can pretend I don't
know where I put it.
I plan to conduct an
extensive search for it,
but tonight I will pray
to the cannibal of souls
who some call Jesus &
beg him not to rise early
& think it's his breakfast.

Electric Snakes

1. Shame *&* tragedy have entered my shabby life. Today I saw another retired professor at the day-old bread store.

2. Fuck these little Minnesota rabbits in my yard. I bought the little shits a bag of baby carrots they chose to spurn. I want the jackrabbits of my youth. Jackrabbits seem only to live west of the Missouri River. Jackrabbits are not rabbits. They are hares. Folks, they come by their name because their huge ears resemble jackass (donkey) ears. So, fuck these Minnesota rabbits. Class dismissed.

3. Here's a headline I yearn to see: "Kanye Caught Cornholing Caitlyn."

4. 75280ZDWIRENONV82. I was the small circle imprisoned inside the steel square. Far away now, thank God, but then, that sultry autumn night on the far cusp of youth with not a single gray hair, yours truly screwed the pooch.

5. Last year there were seven thousand wild Indians or more camped out on the Standing Rock Reservation *&* I thought of Trump's blonde hair *&* I felt the dark wind blowing in from the Little Big Horn. Winter, bleak *&* endless winter is in the air.

Ratiocination

I am a ghost who hates
Rapid City, South Dakota
but I need it occasionally
like a low-dose tweeker
with a weekend habit.
Exiting late Friday mass
at some execrable saloon, I
see some idiot has barfed
a blizzard of gizzards right
next to my shiny, white SUV.
I'm guessing they're gizzards
because the hipster bistro
across the street sells them.
Gizzards from ghost chickens.
Oh, my country…
My country 'tis of thee
sweet land of gizzardry.

Twitchy

for Jim Tate

I can only remember fragments.
I'm OK. My memory is excellent.
My life has been fragments.

Tonight, traveling in an ancient
dream of the American West,
I came upon a ghost town
where ceaseless winds kicked
tumbleweeds down dirt streets
& piled them high against
the clichéd sadness of a gray
wood & woeful world. So,
through the swinging doors
of the saloon went I, wanting
something to wet my whistle.

A stern, white-frocked gunslinger
blocked my path to the bar.
He was a tall drink of water,
but I was stoic & smiling inside,
feeling the loving weight
of a Colt strapped to my side.
"My greatest fear is that I will
lose consciousness when I die
& my second greatest fear is…
that I won't," I told him.

"We shocked your heart back
to a normal sinus rhythm,"
he said. "Get some rest."

I gave him a weak, bitchy smile.
My trigger finger was still twitchy,
but my old fart's heart was not.

Electric Snakes #2

1. America is toxic, & poetry, my minor salvation, my twinkly oasis in the black sky, has become increasingly pointless. So, when I say poets should write poems & otherwise shut the fuck up, I pretend I am not talking to myself.

2. Politics: America elected a lunatic, & greed, as an American core value, shall be worshipped. In other news, the poor will remain poor while wars rage on, & finally, friends, Taco Bell is coming to this small prairie town! Good news, good news.

3. Where have you been published? *Electrical Jekyll, The Jellyroll Review*, and *Web Odes & Oddities*. There are now enough electronic "magazines" so every poet can be published! God bless us one & all.

4. In a thousand years when all the water is gone & our Mother Earth resembles Mars, Facebook will be gone. That is a good thing.

5. Dinner at Mike's Cafe tonight. Liver & onions, mashed potatoes with mushroom gravy, corn, probably canned but not bad, & a cold bottle of Michelob—I don't know why since I've never had Michelob, but it washed the meal down & soothed my hobbling rancor.

Eddie Miles

No doubt, Stephen Curry is brilliant, but who remembers Eddie Miles? In some distant century, Roberto & I roamed the town dump, shooting his .410 at bottles we tossed when I spotted the mangled innards of a Philco radio. I took the broken creature home & pulled the shattered cover off, removed the tubes & took them to the hardware store in town. With new tubes in, it glowed but no sounds came & I saw the antenna was missing so I stuck some rigid copper wire into the slot where the antenna had been & heard human voices. 1962. In our old, ramshackle house on the high desert wastelands, Seattle University basketball bounced into my bedroom from 850 miles to the north. Some cat named Eddie Miles was making shots from every part of that faraway court. The announcer was going wild. "Miles from the corner—Scores!" Miles, whoever he was, scored like a maniac & I just knew he'd score after the game too. As for me, I was still a virgin.

Vanishing

I just had my second cataract surgery
this month. My Third Eye is next.
—Gary David

Whatever became of so-and-so?
Don't know, he just vanished…

Every day people vanish.
Some get abducted by aliens.
Some get erased by cartels.
Some just move to Minnesota.
I am in the process of vanishing.
The first true indicator is music.
Tunes I marched to under flags
of rebellion no longer rock me.
I no longer recognize magic &
in the din of diminished dreams
& whining about money, health,
loneliness & the absence of sex
there are no songs to soothe me.
Anthems of a long-haired youth
now irritate me beyond reason.

It's elementary, my dear Watson.
I am in the process of vanishing.
The second true clue is shadows.
When I sit on the edge of bed,
the nightlight tosses my shadow
against the wall & that's fine
except recently it has been joined
by half a dozen other shadows.

If they could sing I might join
them in their nightly dance,
but they are silent & eerie.
I can ditch the little bastards by
sleeping with all the lights on.
Nevertheless, I continue to be
in the process of vanishing.
It's not the end of the world,
but then again, maybe it is.

The Got-to-Get-Some Blues

My tally is out of whack,
has been for some time now
& truth be known, the actual
tally the past five years is zero.
Hey baby, hey baby, baby,
got me the got-to-get-some blues.

In the treatment room, I close my eyes.
A nurse intrudes: "Are you okay?"
She's a small-town Stevie Nicks.
I tell her yes, that in the closed circle
of brain darkness I can compress time.
I lower my eyes from face to crotch
& she scurries away. I am ridiculous,
but even in illness I am
a dangerous man.

The Succubus of Grief

In a corner of the yard where sand
softened the clay, we planted
deep purple hollyhocks & I
would tease you & call them
ass-biting tarantula flowers.
Twenty-five years later in
my pitch-black bedroom,
I can see those flowers
slither ever so slowly
out of the wall
& up my legs.
I am not sober.
Stone-cold sober, I would
not have become pregnant,
would not have allowed
tarantula venom to take
its toll, would not be
shrieking as ten thousand
baby spiders danced out
of my maudlin heart.

Skinology

Yellow roses, wild roses,
their decades of growth,
a fierce fence between
the drunkenness
of my neighbors
& me.

I have known
some badass Skins.
Clichéd bad-to-the-bone
Indians who were maybe
not bad but just broke,
& broken for sure.

Late winter, late night,
a gentle rapping, a tapping
on my chamber door…
some guy selling a block
of commodity cheese
for five bucks.

You climbed a tree,
sat there for hours
until some kind voice
called you back home.
You unfolded your wings,
took to the air & smashed

into earth. They hauled
you to ER, then Detox
where they laughed
at your broken wings.

Once, I thought
I saw eagles soar,
loop & do the crow hop
in the blue air while
the sun beat the earth
like a drum, but I was
disheveled & drinking
those years.

Indians & the Internet.
Somewhere, sometime.
Whenever a Messiah
Chief is born, jealous
relatives will drag him
down like the old days
only instantly now.

In a brutal land
within a brutal land
with corrupt leaders
& children killing themselves
we know who is to blame.
But, we are on a train,
a runaway train & we
don't know what to do.

The good earth,
the sun blazing down,
us in our chones, butts
stuck in inner tubes,
floating down a mossy
green river, speechless,
stunned silent with joy
& sobriety & youth,
oh youth.

She smiled at me
& got off her horse.
She smelled of leather
& sweat & her kiss has
lasted me fifty years.

Bad Indians do
not go to hell.
They are marched
to the molten core
of the sun & then
beamed back to
their families,
purified, whole
& Holy as hell.

Invisible Places of Refuge

Deep inside myself,
I am running out
of places to hide.
I am an old man,
a dirty old man &
the world we knew
is fading fast away.
I cannot say how I
became covered with
the cobwebs common
to poor & broken folk.
Darling, I cannot say
if I'm spider or fly.

My love, I pray that you
cannot see me now, but
of course you can see me
& yes, I am a walking scar,
one of life's miracles, but
you're just a ghost, still,
the only ghost I
dream hard about.
I will never hide from
the hauntings you offer.

Soon I will need no
invisible places of refuge.
While other spirits float
through a dire dampness
of tears & wet kisses, I
will flitter about, brittle &
arid as a pack of Top Ramen.

Top Ramen is my hemlock.
It shrinks my body & soul.
My carcass has grown thin.
Even my shadow is skeletal.
Embarrassed, it seeks solace
in the dark cells of memory,
but even they are shrinking.

Nevertheless, my dear Gods
of known & unknown ethers...
I thank you for the sweet
& holy miracle of noodles
made from the baked &
pulverized bones of poor folk.

One Day in the Final Week
of a Career in the Academy

Rainy rain *&* I had a headache
from the emails of four Nepali
students who begged for better
grades than their excruciatingly
weak English abilities deserved.
In a nutshell they said: *Professor,*
please consider we tried very hard &
English isn't our primary language.
I said: *This was an English course!*
I appreciate your effort, but I will
not raise the final grades I gave.
They asked to meet. *No can do.*
It was rainy rain outside, so I
assembled some extremely rare
burgers *&* slurped down three
stubby bottles of Red Stripe beer.
I watched Brad Pitt in *A River*
Runs Through It & conjured
fantasies of Montana: brook
trout sizzling in a fry pan *&*
the red hot lips of a succulent,
brown woman kissing me.
Kissing. Me.

Got Those Lonesome Blues
in Small-town Minnesota

I'm awakened by American greed
speeding through prairie night.
There is nothing romantic about
the ghostly howl of Burlington
& Northern Railroad tankers
hauling highly flammable crude
that could incinerate this town.
At midnight in a shotgun shack,
I fear the railway & petroleum
robber barons more than ISIS
& I fear senior citizen loneliness
more than instant immolation.
Darling, I was dreaming of you
when trains pulled me awake
& our wet lips parted ways.
The last time I kissed you
was ten years ago. I shivered
while you slept in your coffin.

The Hermit's Diary

1. Age has withered my rage. The roiling, molten core of my youth has cooled into dull, cold metal. Nevertheless, sometimes I grab a butter knife & dance around the kitchen, threatening the sluggish Mr. Coffee machine.

2. I grew up in a shack. I lived in an 8x10 closet off the front porch of an old railway house: me, my cot, some small shelves on one wall where my mom stacked my clean clothes. I hid out there most days to avoid the cruel, white demon that was my stepfather. I waited in the oppressive air of desert afternoons for him to leave for the swing shift at the copper mine.

   Decades later, I rise in another shack of a house at five in the morning, make coffee, putter around until the early afternoon heat creeps up on me. Then I turn on the air conditioning & go to bed. When I am shivering from the cold, I pull the blankets up & take a nap. I have worked my whole life for such peace.

3. Escaping the glare of the computer, I find myself motoring past my former place of employment. "Itchycoo Park" is playing on the oldies station. I soak up the summertime college mist like an old, dry sponge. Tan girls taking remedial courses are lounging upon the lawns. Firm bottoms & bellies & heads filled with helium. The good ole USA. The euphoric scent of Coppertone simmering on the skin of young women. I inhale the intoxicant as I slowly drive by.

   Cruising past the hospital, I breathe in the hot tar a road crew is laying down. I love the aroma of tar. One desert summer, I worked as a flagman for a paving company. Then, I had a firm bottom & belly. My head was not filled with helium but small, smiling clouds of incinerated flora. 1966.

4. *What will we do there?—We'll get high.*
   What will we touch there?—We'll touch the sky.
      —Small Faces, 1967

Electric Snakes #3

1. In the vertigo of snow. Brain wires are crossed, spitting, hissing. Are these my last minutes or is it merely October wind banging my screen door? Maybe it's witches come to place warts upon my aging face? I fucking detest witches. I do not like their dank bedside manner. I don't like their sour cooking or their ability to change Roquefort into rogue farts.

2. This anonymous email came: "Sooner or later your once-loved body will betray you & you'll swim in a swirling cesspool of decay & disease. It happens to each & every one of us so quit your pitiful public whining."

3. For the past thirty years I have smelled the cheap perfume of the little careerist whores who marched under the banner of literature. Here we go, left, right, left-right, our reeking careers on parade.

4. I live somewhat anonymously in Snowflake, MN: It's got a bad gene pool & is galaxies removed from the real world, but many folks here still understand the concept of manners. It's a million miles from Murderapolis, MN, but very close to North & South Dakota—each one a frozen Mississippi of the High Plains. This town is eerily remote from the real world & quite unbearably white & it seems I am here for the duration.

Brash

Brash is good
but not his kind
my clique agreed.
Calculated & done
for effect only, his
brash was a whore
& not a saintly one
with a heart of gold.
His life seemed contrived.
He leered at the ladies
but lusted (we'd heard)
after young boys & we
never knew if he knew
we knew when his pistol
erupted his brain.

We were not totally
typical academic asshats
& we wanted to be seen
as devoutly collegial, so
even though we really,
really didn't want to,
we figured it would be
good karma to visit
his hospital bed so
we went, but he didn't
know us & we did not
know him. He was no
longer brash & never
would be again.

We nodded, shrugged
our way to our cars &
sped off into the night
with unspoken plans
to subdue the coldest
martinis in town.

Homeland Security

Dredged in the sourness of morning
& fried in the ambience of poverty,
I opened the door & beheld Mormon boys.
They said soft, strange words to me.
I crossed my eyes & wiggled my tongue.
They left quickly & I stood in my underwear,
surveying my neighborhood.
It was secure once again.

When You Have White Hair

When you have white hair,
love is like the phantom
pain of a lost limb.

When you have white hair,
love is a memory
of a memory.
A rattle of leaves
in an autumn brain.

When you have white hair,
your ancient nether
regions are blanketed
with either snow or cobwebs.
It creeps out vital folks.

When you have white hair,
you are truly fucked
& never fucked.

The One

They come to me in dreams,
the ones I wanted, the ones
I had, even ones I invented
out of pure loneliness. But,
there is one who is the only one.
She was sweet & tart as buckberries
& tawny as the dry soil that grew us.
She had the coal-black hair of our race
& green eyes that wobbled my knees.
Some days I can't recall her looks.
For fifty years I have waited
for her to enter my dreams,
but she never has, she
never has & I think
I know why, but
that is a secret
I will take to
our shallow
grave.

Dragon Slayer

My once-shining sword is bent & dull.
In my youth, we collaborated & slew
a thousand flaming dragons.
Now I can only battle
beasts with my tongue.
"Come here," I say.
"Let me whisper some
delirious secrets to you."
They get all wide-eyed
& lie still & listen—then
I attack from the back.
I am a foolish but not
too foolish old man.
The dragons giggle
& fly fast away.

Monstrosities

1. Finally, I have become unsalvageable. The very concept of America is a ghost to the ghost-boy who once uttered *¡Viva la Revolución!* Today I slathered two pieces of dried Wonder Bread with "I Can't Believe It's Not Butter" *&* made me a monstrous cold beef stew sandwich. Where is Mario Batali or Mario Savio when I really need them?

2. Today I told Bob, my good Republican doctor, that since a monster has been elected to lead us, I'd need an Rx for medical monsterjuana. The Beemer-driving medic gave a silly grin, thinking I was making some kind of lame joke. No siree, Bob, I was not.

3. My prescription seems
   like the strictures of Zion.
   Damn, Dr. Bob says
   I cannot eat greens.
   No potatoes, no salt,
   no chocolate it seems.
   No blood-red tomatoes
   that I've held so dear.
   No Coke, no bananas
   & no foaming beer.
   No Pepsi or coffee
   & no more cheesecake.
   He might as well ship
   my sad ass to Salt Lake.

Prairie Madness

Box my bone ash. FedEx me to my high desert home. Toss me high into the coyote air; let me dust the sage & horny toads. I refuse to sleep under this alien soil, this Minnesota moonscape, this cold cheese land devoid of sane hills & trees. Fuck this flat world of poisonous cornfields & ceaseless wind. This abominable prairie wind. This divine wind of madness. This rapist wind.

A brassy woman materialized last week one block from me. She's made of bronze with billowing skirt & windblown bonnet. She's a pioneer woman, a settler woman, the kind of woman who ran from her sod house & stinking husband & ceaseless wind, ran to the Indians who always seemed calm. I walked by her last night & tweaked her à la Trump. She remained dead calm. I ran home & chopped off my hand.

The Motherland

Pallid folks, both guided
& misguided, bump uglies
& exchange vows against
a backdrop of dirges sung
by millions of dark men
seething behind steel bars.
Pallid folks are bored with
the old songs of pain & are
thankful that the cold heart
of democracy, sliced thinly,
has fed them for centuries.
Sieg Heil, Mama-jammers.
Sieg Heil, Flim-flammers.

—*Election Night, 2016*

Electric Snakes #4

1. I inject the pallid, shared sadness of Facebook until it tangles my eyeballs. My addiction to it is lessening, but I'd better say something because I haven't posted anything in a month & six people have sent me notes asking if I was still among the living. I think I am still alive, but alive in Minnesota is a slow death. This is the frozen land of the dull & the dead. Dull & dead earth, dull & dead humanity, dull & dead weather. I type out "Minnesota sucks the scrotum of Satan" and post it.

2. I had to drive a "friend" to Sioux Falls airport & this "friend" just had to listen to *Prairie Home Companion*. This meant a painful hour & a half of biting my lip. Garrison Keillor doesn't translate into the 21st century. Back in the day, I used to have friends who listened to this creature, but they all died. Actually, Keillor is probably dead too, but it's hard to distinguish a zombie from the average Minnesota asshat.

3. I boasted that if the tangerine Mussolini were elected president, I was moving to rural Colorado to live out my few remaining years searching hard for rigid & righteously beauteous gluteus through the constant veil of ganja. But, I am too old to face a new move. The aging process does contain ample foolishness. I am talking to a toe I may soon lose.

4. Nor could I move to New Mexico & gobble red or green chile every day & score the ganja from senior citizen gangsters...white-haired, hardcore Gs with walkers...Los Viejos Veteranos, Santa Fe, NM Chapter.

5. But ghosts in the Great Basin are insistently calling me home. What to do, what to do with my ancient body. A soot-black locomotive is roaring through my brain. The ghost-whistle of memory is excruciating & lovely.

6. The humbuggery of our lives: What to do, what to do? What the holy hell to do & then the torrential tremors of how & why? O knees of creak. O back of stoop. O big toe, do not desert me before my final pilgrimage.

Mom

Jesus died for somebody's sin, but not mine.
—Patti Smith

My old body shuffles absently
through these cluttered rooms.
I'm older than you when you died.

Owl murmur weaves through
a shaky, dark wind tonight.
There is so much unsaid.

Your muted love was never
enough to fill jagged wounds,
turned now to lovely scars.

I am exiled to a frozen land,
but the winter sun lightens
my scars, rekindles my love

& I am a smiling child again.
This is no convenient copout
& not a classical suppression.

Dear Mom, the sun is afire
like the place I suspect we will
meet up at. I love you still.

A Reasonable Nightmare

Underneath the piñon pine,
a soft bed of fragrant needles.
Down in the valley, a crystal
clear creek with fat rainbows
waiting to jump in a skillet.
No wolves or bears here & no
people, except for one & she
is misty & incredibly pretty,
dressed as she was while
she slept in her coffin.
Her eyes are milky & her
once-red lips are withered.
I tell her I am not afraid.
"Let me join you," I say
& she shakes her head *No*.
I awaken afraid & shivering
in my unreasonable bed
in my unreasonable nation.
Tonight I will ask her again.

Electric Snakes #5

Home, whatever home was. I cannot go there. Most boyhood friends are dead, desiccated by the blood-drying wind. The high desert wind. I hear them moaning, moaning my name & things I dare not speak aloud. I thought once I slouched past sixty-five, I'd be free to say anything. Any fucking thing I wanted to. But that's not the way it's come to be. Today, I shot an arrow into my foot. I said, "Sarah, you're everything I could ask for. But I'm too damn ancient to ask." Flabbergasted & hurt, Sarah booked. Boot-scooted out of my feeble life. My words saved her from my disintegrating self. She is free, free & not just another sordid tale spun by a flaccid Ulysses.

You Say You Are Indian

You say you are Indian.
You don't look it, but
then who am I to say?
Someone once told me
the way to find if someone
is Indian is to walk past
them & turn around quickly.
If they have done the same
& you find them staring
into your eyeball then
they are Indian.

You say you are Indian.
You don't look it, but
then who am I to say?
If you are Indian then
you're from that tribe
where men have little ones
& the women have big ones
& lady, you have a whopper.
A veritable snapping turtle.
Damn right you are Indian.
Anything you say, just
quit snapping those
fearsome jaws.

Electric Snakes #6

The baked morning dawned & Satan's stomach was filled with angry, cross-eyed cobras. Bad tacos. Taco John's tacos. He woke to the fleeting thought he'd died & gone to Hell, a place he'd run from so long ago. He got up & seated himself upon the porcelain throne & found CNN on his iPad. That orange shit-goblin who'd once been his acolyte was cranking out massive lies from his tiny, reptilian brain. Satan shrugged & Googled "best tacos in America." Why he just didn't teleport to Mexico is unclear.

Coyotes

On a stark, sandy hill
two coyotes danced
furry ear to furry ear,
attempting the tango
in timid moonlight.

Seated at the kitchen table
two hours later, they both
began to howl over some
minor calamity, some
failed disambiguation,
but soon they blubbered
& came to their senses
in a calm recollection
of their dance & the moon
& the fact that they would
never even consider ripping
each other's furry throats
if they gave up the bottle.

Electric Snakes #7

I loved your poems…on paper. But when I heard you read, emoting in that sing-song "poetry" voice, my faith in our race was shattered. I was expecting a grassroots, hardcore voice & I felt betrayed. I guess I was hoping you would sound like a chain-smoking, whiskey-guzzling amazon, your throat raspy from kissing far too many tattooed ladies. *I can sometimes be a cruel creature, a monster.*

But America itself has always been a monster. We like to pretend we can't see that & keep our monstrous nature hidden like a Sasquatch in the deepest, dank forest. Now, since the election, pale Nazi monsters strut upon our sidewalks in broad daylight & all I can do is shake my withered head & curse them from time to time. How do we fight in a land led by a moral invalid?

Metaphorical Winter Obituary

Everything is everything, we
used to say back in the day.
My feet were dead twigs
poking into December snow.
My yard was not really my yard,
but a frozen mirror of death.
At -20 below Satan's bratwurst
would shrivel into something
resembling a Vienna sausage.
Still I skated forward & almost
made it inside but the brutal
witches of winter shanked me
with their brutal ice-breasts.
I froze & shattered into cubes
that somehow found their way
into a massive gin & tonic.

Electric Snakes #8

'Twas the season of the baby Jesus & way up north the reindeer were pouty. None of these ruminants liked Rudolph because he had the big, red nose of an alkie (since he was one) & he'd pulled a lot of crappy moves when smashed. But then one eve of Christmas dawned & it was really freaking foggy. Ever-forgiving St. Nick, who'd had a few himself, said, "Bro, will you lead this expedition by the beacon of your bulbous proboscis?" Thus, Rudolph went down in history & later down on Mrs. Claus & from that time onward the other reindeer let him join their games, checkers, cribbage, strip poker, I don't know exactly what deer do, but it was all good. Though the exact date this happened is unclear, it was certainly years before Santa got busted for elf molestation.

Christmas: Sixty-Six & Alone

Up at six I brewed coffee
& opened my one present
to myself this year.
A fine Harry & David
fruitcake ordered online.
I don't know why folks
make fun of fruitcakes.
I cut me a large Christmas
slice to go with my coffee.
Yuck. I spat out the first
bite & rinsed my mouth
with near-scalding coffee.
I went back to bed & slept
deeply until noon & then
arose to brew more coffee.
The TV weatherwoman said
a storm was on the way & we
might get six inches of snow.
"Six inches would be lovely
on Christmas Day," she said.
Yes, that is what she said
& for the second time
that holy day, hot coffee
spewed from my mouth.
Nothing to do but go back to bed.

Reaper Don't Scare Me

Seasons don't fear the reaper.
Nor do wind, the sun or the rain.
　　—Blue Oyster Cult

Tonight I pray
the obese snow does
not accordion my house,
but at least the squawking
of this prairie town is silenced
& the white noise of memory
takes its place.

When I was eleven, Jack,
an older, browner cousin
told me the cruel footsteps
of the Reaper are muted
when fat, fluffy snowflakes
blind the eyes of the world.
"Lock up all your doors,"
he said. "Don't sit close
to any damn windows."

"Girl I used to know," he said.
"Married a big, white guy
who worked swing shift at
the Anaconda copper mine.
Foreman for the primary
& secondary ore crushers.
He was good to her & got
her anything she wanted,
but she was a crazy girl &

got herself an Indian lover.
She'd take him to her bed
while her husband worked.
One night they sat at a table
next to a window, the shade
pulled against the night.
They were sharing a pint
of Old Crow whiskey when
a 12-gauge shotgun blasted
the window into a blizzard
of glass, exploded my left
eyeball & instantly ended
some Indian love. Shit,
who knows? A dozen guys
said the husband had been
at work the whole night
& never left for a minute.
Nobody was ever arrested
& I became One-eyed Jack,
but I beat The Reaper."

It's night & fat, fluffy
snowflakes have carpeted
my house & I'm wondering
whatever became of One-eyed
Jack, my faraway cousin & I
say a prayer for his missing eye
that saw love & then blackness.

Valentine

Sweet, unbridled lust
shimmered past my door.
It shimmied in the corner
of my eyeballs & when I
looked up, it was gone.
It was oval like the focal
point of a searchlight
except it was black.

These years I sit
in golden sunshine
& pray the orb above
might turn black, too.
That I might turn back to you.

Hoping to Run into Clark

Gray clouds smother
the once garish colors
of my comic book life.
I drive my gray matter
through the Iowa sky
that has fallen to earth
turning tasseled corn gray.
A psychedelic archeologist,
mired in graying decrepitude,
I am searching for the gray
graves of Jonathan *&* Ma Kent.
Maybe I will run into their
eternally mourning son *&*
plead with him to wake
the fuck up *&* move past
retirement *&* eradicate
the blond, greasy fop
who is more Mussolini
than a new Lex Luthor.

Resurgence

The burgeoning warmth
of a brilliant April sun
tricks a foolish forsythia
to rise over feeble snow.
In an alternate universe,
the new king is wailing
on his throne of thorns
in his huge, golden palace.
Behind his back, his zombie
retinue skulks *&* ponders
a full, frontal retreat.

A Flickering Candle Prayer

You cannot petition the Lord with prayer.
  —Jim Morrison

The candle flickered,
demanded I speak
the unspeakable in
the sad, fading light.
O Lord in Heaven, I
now confess I
had no choice but to
piss on that fabled
flickering candle.
It's better to live
in darkness than
to burn in heaven.
Amen.

Vacuity

I am soaring serenely, an eagle
with not one feather of irony.
Then my engine stalls & I
nose-dive into the rising earth.
I pierce our mother & swim
through deep, dank soil, but
freeze when Wovoka's bones
ghost-dance eerily toward me.
I ask the prophet why he's here
under Great Plains & not resting
eternally in stoic Schurz, NV.
"I'm here to kill a black snake,"
he says & I ask him *huh*, but
he simply shrugs & runs away
fast without answering me.
What the holy hell is this
dead world coming to?

The Equivocator

In another century there
was one week I told two
different Indian women
I loved them with
all my heart & I think
I did truly love both.
But when I was young
my dick always lied to
my heart & my foolish,
lonely heart believed it all.
Nevertheless, I loved both
& after thirty years still do.
One is dead & the other is
fat & married with four
strapping sons, none
of them mine, but
Jesus Christ I
wish they were.

Electric Snakes #9

When the angel Lucifer fell from God's grace, I'm sure he plummeted gracefully & landed on his feet. Nevertheless, he landed in the precincts of Hell. When I slipped on the ice in my driveway, I came smashing down, face-first into frozen Hell, though the local folk call it Minnesota. I could not get up & flailed on the mirror of ice. A neighbor lady salting her steps shook her old head in disgust like I was drunk so when I finally arose & staggered inside I made some strong coffee & spiked it with Jameson.

Sicangu Winyan

Don't...turn on me...baby.
I am an old man & my heart
is paper-thin like Zhivago's.
Your ruby lips make me blush
when they touch my ears & sing
the dark-soiled songs the creature
named America cannot comprehend.
If this is love, it is an ancient love.
If you are a ghost then I am too
& if I am a ghost, there's no need
to spend my social security
on those magic blue pills
that might glue us together.

The Mirage of Memory

If there is a certain smell,
a certain taste, a wondrous
occasion you wish to return to,
poetry will allow you to do that,
a noted poet told me forty years ago.

Then, I thought the concept of a time
machine made of words was such
utter bullshit. I still do. How can
you grasp a glimpse of past
passion when you can't
recall who you had
for breakfast?

What the Christ was it?
Hot eggs or cold pizza & why
does America continually forget
its genocide of Indian peoples?
Now I remember. Donuts.
America. White dough
with a hole in the middle.

Electric Snakes #10

1. The Monosyllabic Yam is a blowhard, a polished equivocator, but I believe a coward resides in his heart. I believe he is a container for the bitterness many people grow as they transition from middle age to old age. He would have had no qualms about leading this nation into a nuclear war. It would be like baby's blood to a vampire.

2. In the mist of pain, a clarity comes & says I am here now, at that pot at the end of a rainbow, but the pot is not filled with gold. It is filled with me & water, boiling water & leering cannibal elves are dancing & drooling, shimmying & slobbering & then the sweet Elysium of medicinal herb kicks in. It's all good & gooder.

3. In the Barnes & Noble I retreated behind some stacks & released into the air a creature of methane & dying onion & out of nowhere the most beautiful woman in the peculiar village of Sioux Falls was smiling, standing next to me. I looked at the shelves of poetry & understood no book there could save me.

4. Hermeneutics: The dance moves of Herman Munster.

5. When someone dies, it is perfectly permissible to yank them from their coffin, stand them up & walk them around the room like you would do for someone who is drunk on their ass. Sometimes it revives them. Sometimes it doesn't.

6. There is a raisin in every grape. There is no sane reason for rape. Treason lives in the grape & dark seasons will live in

the rape. They fed us the fruit of the vine & we signed their fucking treaties.

7. Plump cows meandered east to west, mooing, covering the land with shit & smiling at their plan to assassinate the buffalo.

8. The creature squatting upon the throne has no soul. The throne the creature squats upon has no hole. The resultant miasma poisons the land & the two red dragonflies coupling in mid-air do not care at all.

The Imposition of Order in Minnesota

All lawns must be mowed frequently.
Consider dandelions to be agents of ISIS.
The humid air shall be sliced into cubes
twenty feet tall and twenty feet wide.
Each house will be assigned one cube.
Each house shall have two elm trees &
a hedgerow made of yellow roses.
Each rose will be assigned two bees.
Each house shall have enough
insecticide to kill two bees.

Electric Snakes #11

An onion. So, a Vidalia onion on death row broke free of its mesh bag of confinement & slithered into a corner of the kitchen counter where for some strange reason I pile used plastic bags. It hid there for several weeks, trembling in its newfound freedom, before it made a decision to give itself up to me. It waved a green flag of surrender. When I noticed it, it had four bright green shoots rising ten inches into the air. I don't think anyone wants a pregnant onion on their kitchen counter, so I decided to throw it out into my backyard where stupid little rabbits lurk. But, a light snow was falling & it was only ten degrees out. It would freeze to death before the rabbits found it & ate it. I gently stroked its green shoots and set it back on the counter. These mornings now I say hi to it when I make my morning coffee. In three or four weeks the gray world outside will start turning green.

Magpie in Margaritaville

A shimmer of green
floats off the glossy
black feathers as he
raises his sharp beak
to speak. "I piss on you
& your pithy depictions
of woe & woe unto you
who lack spirit guides.
You have made careers
on the backs of red folk.
Do not for an instant
pretend you know me
when you cannot see
that my feathers are red."

One Night in Sioux Falls

SUV was too tall for ATM
so my aging body exited
to collect the green, but
a meth-lit motherfucker
materialized next to me
& his pimply mouth said,
"Gimme that cash, fucker."
I jumped in my vehicle &
locked the doors & he stood
there, perplexed & shaking.
I stuck out my tongue, put
my thumbs in my ears
& wiggled my fingers.
Then I hit my loud horn
& he bolted into the night.
I started the car & followed
him, beeping & beeping.
Bored with glorious cruelty,
I headed to Drive-In Liquors
for a half pint of sedation &
after two healthy glugs pointed
my car north towards the lonely
& toxic Minnesota cornfields.

The Questioning

On a quiet street
where old ghosts meet
I see her walking now...
    —Patrick Kavanagh

When the summer sun
staggered *&* fell blindly
into the horizon, the crows
in our elms ceased cawing.
We stared at the auburn
sunset *&* without bickering
acknowledged, agreed sky
was the powdered blood
of our ancestors, returned
to blanket our lives, lives
beyond their comprehension.
Embraced in the soft warmth
of South Dakota night, we
vowed to each other that
we knew who *&* what we
were *&* our love was what
we really wanted, but one
of us became an infidel,
a traitor to love *&* home.

What do we really want?
Why, when offered a sweet
life, do some of us seek out
a taste of fatal bitterness?
Sometimes the spotlight

of sunshine brings forth
our pallid confessions,
but we still don't know
why we eat each day &
turn it into starless night.
We gobble ravenously this
diet of gleeful darkness &
we do not know whether
the sky is filled with crows
or crows are filled with sky.
We subsist on the futile
& bloodless questioning
of the carrion of memory.

I accept my racial duality
as I accept the fact that
some scared little shit
spent my life sneering
at clouds & taunting God
on his marshmallow couch.
When the clouds turned black
& the hard rains fell, he opened
my mouth wide until it filled
& made me spit the rain back
up into the questioning sky
& the feather-wet crows in
the cottonwoods cursed me.

It comes to me like headlights
that startle, freeze a deer on

a highway at night, but I'm
alone in bed when blinding
memories strike, bound into
one, all those little cruelties &
all those immature, uncaring
moments when yours truly
was a no good son of a bitch.
So what can be done about it
now with her in the ground
for the ten short minutes that
grew into ten long years & me
on the slow road to join her?
I wish I had answers for each
dead deer being dined upon
by the sleek, cackling crows &
all their flesh-tearing questions.

The Day They Set the Dogs upon the Water Protectors

Ensconced in torpor
in a demimonde of corn,
the hero stood before
the flame, its rivulets
of smoke arching skyward.
He was languidly inhaling
Coors & grilling bratwurst.
And then it happened. For
the second time in a week,
he was shaken from lassitude
by the thuggish fluttering of
a dark, whispering wind.
Evil ghosts had broached
his mundane inner sanctum.
Custer's shit-stained saddle
tramps had risen & were
haunting the plains again.

Lamentation

She was tarnished now,
no longer the shining star
in the galaxy of my youth.
I slipped her panties down…
Skid marks! Vicious ones.
The schoolboy in me blanched.
Demons danced everywhere.
It was The End of Days.
I pulled up my pants
& backed out of her trailer.
The night sky was aflame.
I was suddenly an old man.
with earth crumbling under my feet.

Electric Snakes #12

A winter's tale. A couple of nights ago it was -27 below. Because old men have the right to sleep any time they want, I hit the hay at 7:00 p.m. My bed is one of my few pleasures. I live alone. I pulled the clean sheets, blanket, & quilt up over me & turned on my left side to dream. The pillow was off-kilter. I reached under my head & pulled it about eight inches closer. I snuggled & I yawned, but just then someone pulled the pillow back down about eight inches—pulled it harshly. I live alone so I slept with the television on & awoke to an odious shit-goblin being sworn into our highest office. Friends, it's morning but the sun is setting. The sun is setting & incomprehensible evil is rising.

The Photograph

Inside his hairy cave,
the hermit casts a lonely
shadow upon the wall.
His bored shadow wants
to wrestle, but he does not.
His shadow always wins &
then has its way with him.
The hermit is damn tired
of a life on life's bottom.
He reaches into his wallet
& retrieves her photograph
& holds it near the flicker
of his campfire, hoping
she too will dance upon
the wall, but her choice
is to sit this one out.
The ghosts of the past
are often cruel or simply
bored by being beckoned.

Electric Snakes #13

In the Legion bar. This turdbucket of a town. A drunken rube is bending my ears about the carved rock Minnesota folks have named the "Kensington Runestone." This dude says this rock proves Vikings were here. That they journeyed to this forlorn state centuries before the killer Columbus.

Small snakes inside my brain hiss *&* roll their eyes. Par for the course. This *is* a town of Republican vegetables. But OK, let's say back in the day, way, way back in the ancient mists of time, Vikings did break out of throat-slitting lethargy to discover *&* lay claim to Minnesota. No other folk were around. Yes, of course, Indians were around, but they just blended into the trees, contented with astrology, fine wines *&* endless games of Space Invaders. The Indians never really feared the serenity-crashing, Nordic horde. It was more a case of good sense over bad scents. But, to cover their asses they cursed all future lovers of Norsemen *&* vowed to make them cry every autumn in the ugly Twin Cities. Thus, last Sunday when the Vikings traveled to Green Bay, they got their lame purple asses ruined. Stoned.

In Lieu of a Communion Wafer

More often than not
growing up in poverty
extinguishes any sense
of irony, but our humor
(often it's a cruel humor)
abounds & saves, yeah,
it abounds & saves us
like a big, fat frybread
saves a watery soup.

The Tinderbox

The parched land was brittle
& the local paper said it was
a tinderbox though I doubt
any there could sketch one.
It was metaphor, a semantic
misfire much like the words
of the alcoholic medicine man
who had long ago sold his soul.
He prayed to the rain to come
when he should have prayed
to the cloud nation. Clouds
are the landlords of wetness.
But, maybe out of pity, they
came, towering thunderheads
spitting lightning & no rain.
His wife shook her head,
scowled & then wept,
wept for her people
& what they'd become.

To the Nude Tending Tomatoes
a Little Northwest of Town

Increasingly, my pen holds no blood
& I scribble my tales in mayonnaise.
I was once a mean motor scooter.
Now I'm just an old coot
with a haphazard
yen for cooter, but
I love your tomatoes,
sweet & succulent, sliced
thickly on soft white bread
with mayo & lots of pepper.
An old man often confuses
tomatoes & love & lust,
though each in its own
time withers & rots.

Grilled Cheese & Tomato Soup

After midnight on these plains
& they say a blizzard is coming.
Twitchy insomnia & the sleeping
pill of television is not working.
Fox News is playing their recap
of the latest mass shooting &
some dickless talking head
from the NRA is offering up
the predictable smokescreen,
a variation of "it's not cars
that kill people—it's the nut
behind the wheel."

But the gun nuts lack nuts
& I despise them even though
in this 21st century, in this small
& sleepy Minnesota college town,
I sleep with a .45 Kimber 1911
on my nightstand & I'd probably
fire if a knife-holding-meth-fueled
fuckwad materialized near my bed.
That is what my brave brain says
to my shivering, cowardly heart
& my eyes see me, sad & confined
to a small room, awaiting execution
when I spot the bedroom window
in the house I grew up in & climb
out, find my bike and pedal through
wheatfields as tall as my shoulder—
how did the wheat grow so tall &

how long will it take me to pedal
to Chicago where I plan to live
the life of a normal but very
anonymous refugee?

Sometime enemies inhabit my dreams,
but I remain pleasant & fight the urge
to call them demons as they saunter
around, then become bored & leave.
The dismal landscape of the dream
awakens me to midnight's simple
pleasures: a Velveeta grilled cheese
& a steaming cup of tomato soup.
The snow is deeper than dreamed
wheat & I could be the last man
on this silent earth, savoring
the promised & final feast
of a condemned man.

Scene from a Movie about Life in a Small Minnesota Hamlet

This half-breed Indian smashed his vehicle. No need to be taken to the hospital since I crashed into the damned hospital! Had an appointment, pulled into a parking space & (my story is) the fucking accelerator stuck. Cue those old Batman sound effects. Ka-Boom! Ka-Pow! Add some minor bumps & bruises & a major butt-ache for my insurance guy. In decrepitude I am still moving forward. Behold me now, cruising this bright-white Minnesota village by taxi, as regal as any half-breed Indian you ever saw.

Electric Snakes #14

1. An ancient man crawls out of bed *&* enters the world the wrong way *&* twists his trick knee. His goddamned knee hurts like a son of a son of a bitch, so he is full-on cantankerous…his faith dissolved. Today he will not do the pony like Bony Moronie even if he could remember how.

2. Yesterday the new meds made me think I had lost my marbles, but last night I dreamed I was walking down a dusty road, my jeans pockets bulging with my long lost Taws, Cats-eyes, Dobies, Steelies, Aggies, Puries *&* Pee-wees. I awoke with a raging boner. The first time in many years. Let all old men dream of marbles. The strange medicine of miniature planets.

3. On the silver screen, I saw Indians peering in grimy saloon windows while the crooked sheriff frolicked upstairs with a dancehall whore. I left the theater *&* I peered into a local saloon. My mother saw me *&* waved. I was ten years old *&* craved the Lucky Strikes *&* Lucky Lager she so loved.

4. On eBay I spot a toy top, not a string one, but the painted-tin plunger type, from Japan, the kind we spun in Great Basin dirt, the top that spun me sixty years into the future, the machine I will ride back into the whirling chasm of birth.

ABOUT THE AUTHOR

A half-breed Indian, Adrian C. Louis was born in Nevada and is an enrolled member of the Lovelock Paiute Tribe. From 1984–97, Louis taught at Oglala Lakota College on the Pine Ridge Reservation. Earlier, he edited four Native newspapers, including *The Lakota Times*. Louis recently retired as Professor of English at the Minnesota State University in Marshall. He has written fourteen books of poems and two works of fiction: *Wild Indians & Other Creatures*, short stories, and *Skins*, a novel. *Skins* was produced as a feature film in 2002. Louis has won various writing awards, including Pushcart Prizes and writing fellowships from the National Endowment for the Arts, the Bush Foundation, and the Lila Wallace Foundation. His most recent collection of poems is *Random Exorcisms* (Pleiades Press, 2016). Website: www.Adrian-C-Louis.com

Ω

CPSIA information can be obtained
at www.ICGtesting.com
Printed in the USA
LVHW030750030821
694341LV00001B/15

9 781935 218913